To

_____

From

_____

365 DAY BRIGHTENERS

FOR My SISTER My FRIEND

365 Day Brighteners™ For My Sister, My Friend

© 2003 DaySpring Cards, Inc.
Published by Garborg's®, a brand of DaySpring Cards, Inc.
Siloam Springs, Arkansas

Scripture quotations are from the following sources:
The HOLY BIBLE, NEW INTERNATIONAL VERSION ® (NIV) ®
© 1973, 1978, 1984 by International Bible Society. Used by permission of Zondervan Publishing House. The Holy Bible, New Century Version (NCV) © 1987, 1988, 1991 by Word Publishing, Dallas, Texas 75039. Used by permission. THE MESSAGE © Eugene H. Peterson 1993, 1994, 1995. Used by permission of NavPress Publishing Group. All rights reserved. The Living Bible (TLB) © 1971 by permission of Tyndale House Publishers, Inc., Wheaton, IL.

Except for Scripture verses, references to men and masculine pronouns have been replaced with "people," "women," and gender-neutral or feminine pronouns.

ISBN 1-58061-737-9   Printed in China

365 DAY BRIGHTENERS

BRIGHTENERS

For My Sister My Friend

GARBORG'S®

because every day is a gift

$\mathcal{L}$ooking forward into
an empty year strikes one with
a certain awe, because one finds
therein no recognition. The years
behind have a friendly aspect, and
they are warmed by the fires we
have kindled, and all their
echoes are the echoes
of our own voices.

ALEXANDER SMITH

JANUARY 1

JANUARY 2

*T*he comfort of knowing
that our bond will survive despite
our differences and that our
connection provides each of us with
a more accurate picture of ourselves
enhances our chances of finding
inner peace and satisfaction
as we age together.

JANE MERSKY LEDER

$\mathcal{L}$ove doesn't try to
see through others,
but to see others through.

JANUARY 3

JANUARY 4

*P*erhaps you'd be a bit
surprised how often, if you knew,
A joke, a song, a memory
will make me think of you.
It's like another moment that
we've really spent together,
Reminding me a sister is a
friend who's there forever.

*T*wo are better than one,
because they have a good
reward for their toil. For if they fall,
one will lift up the other.

ECCLESIASTES 4:9-10 NRSV

JANUARY 5

JANUARY 6

$\mathcal{A}$ candle loses nothing of its
light by lighting another candle.

$\mathcal{M}$ay God's richest blessings
be upon you both today and throughout
the year—and may those blessings
flow through you to touch the lives
of everyone you meet.

GARY SMALLEY

JANUARY 7

JANUARY 8

*T*hough we travel the
world over to find what is
beautiful, we must carry it within
us or we find it not.

$\mathcal{W}$hen you are lonely I wish you love;
When you are down I wish you joy;
When you are troubled I wish you peace;
When things are complicated I wish
you simple beauty;
When things are chaotic I wish
you inner silence;
When things seem empty I wish you hope.

JANUARY 9

JANUARY 10

How precious it is, Lord, to
realize that you are thinking about
me constantly! I can't even count
how many times a day your
thoughts turn towards me.

PSALM 139:17 TLB

$\mathcal{S}$o much of what we learn
of love we learn at home.

JANUARY 11

JANUARY 12

$\mathcal{T}$he highest love of all finds
its fulfillment not in what it keeps,
but in what it gives.

FATHER ANDREW

$\mathcal{F}$or there is no friend like a sister
In calm or stormy weather;
To cheer one on the tedious way,
To fetch one if one goes astray,
To lift one if one totters down,
To strengthen whilst one stands.

<small>CHRISTINA ROSSETTI</small>

JANUARY 13

JANUARY 14

*T*reat people as if they were
what they should be, and you help
them become what they are
capable of becoming.

GOETHE

$\mathcal{M}$ay you be given more
and more of God's kindness,
peace, and love.

JUDE 1:2 TLB

JANUARY 15

JANUARY 16

Love, like sunshine's warmth,
beams forth on every side
and bends to every need.

*T*here will be days which
are great and everything goes
as planned. There will be other days
when we aren't sure why we got out of
bed. Regardless of which day it is, we
can be assured that God takes
care of our daily needs.

EMILIE BARNES

JANUARY 17

JANUARY 18

Happy times and bygone days are never lost.... In truth, they grow more wonderful within the heart that keeps them.

KAY ANDREW

$\mathcal{W}$e know that trouble is a part of life. If you don't share it, you don't give the person who loves you a chance to love you enough. And sister, that's me.

JANUARY 19

JANUARY 20

*M*ay you always be doing
those good, kind things which show
you are a child of God, for this
will bring much praise and
glory to the Lord.

PHILIPPIANS 1:11 TLB

$\mathcal{W}$hat the heart gives
away is never lost...it is kept in
the hearts of others.

JANUARY 21

JANUARY 22

Family lifts our spirits and sticks
with us when times are tough.

*G*od can use a small match
to light a great torch.

JANUARY 23

JANUARY 24

*I*nsomuch as anyone pushes
you nearer to God, she is your
truest friend.

$\mathcal{L}$et us love, not in word or
speech, but in truth and action.

1 JOHN 3:18 NRSV

JANUARY 25

JANUARY 26

By now we know and anticipate one another so easily, so deeply, we unthinkingly finish each other's sentences, and often speak in code. No one else knows what I mean so exquisitely, painfully well; no one else knows so exactly what to say, to fix me.

JOAN FRANK

$\mathcal{W}$e are sisters.
We will always be sisters.
Our differences may
never go away, but neither,
for me, will our song.

ELIZABETH FISHEL

JANUARY 27

JANUARY 28

Love grows by giving.
The love we give away is the
only love we keep. The only way
to retain love is to give it away.

$\mathcal{T}$hen come the wild weather,
come sleet or snow,
We will stand by each other,
however it blow.

SIMON DACH

JANUARY 29

JANUARY 30

*L*et us outdo each other in
being helpful and kind to each other
and in doing good.

HEBREWS 10:24 TLB

$\mathcal{T}$hose who bring sunshine
into the lives of others cannot
keep it from themselves.

SIR JAMES M. BARRIE

JANUARY 31

FEBRUARY 1

*W*e have been in God's
thought from all eternity, and in
His creative love, His attention
never leaves us.

MICHAEL QUOIST

$\mathcal{F}$amilies give us
many things—love and meaning,
purpose and an opportunity
to give, and a sense of humor.

FEBRUARY 2

FEBRUARY 3

We know one another's faults, virtues, catastrophes, mortifications, triumphs, rivalries, desires, and how long we can each hang by our hands to a bar. We have been banded together under pack codes and tribal laws.

ROSE MACAULAY

God has given each of you
some special abilities; be sure
to use them to help each other,
passing on to others God's many
kinds of blessings.

1 Peter 4:10 TLB

FEBRUARY 4

FEBRUARY 5

What shall I bestow upon a friend?... Laughter to sustain when sorrow may bring pain, a bright song of life, a belief that winter ends in the glory of spring, and a prayer of hope for peace that will forever stay.

LEA PALMER

One can never consent to
creep when one feels an
impulse to soar.

HELEN KELLER

FEBRUARY 6

FEBRUARY 7

*O*ur joy will be complete if
we remain in His love—for His love
is personal, intimate, real, living,
delicate, faithful love.

MOTHER TERESA

$\mathcal{A}$ sister can be seen as
someone who is both ourselves
and very much not ourselves—
a special kind of double.

TONI A. H. MCNARON

FEBRUARY 8

FEBRUARY 9

*L*et him have all your worries
and cares, for he is always thinking
about you and watching everything
that concerns you.

1 PETER 5:7 TLB

I said a prayer for you today
And I know God must have heard,
I felt the answer in my heart
Although He spoke no word....
I asked for happiness for you
In all things great and small,
But it was His loving care
I prayed for most of all.

FEBRUARY 10

FEBRUARY 11

*Y*ou are a creation
of God unequaled anywhere
in the universe.... Thank Him for
yourself and then for all the rest
of His glorious handiwork.

NORMAN VINCENT PEALE

$\mathcal{T}$he older you get
the more you realize
that kindness is synonymous
with happiness.

LIONEL BARRYMORE

FEBRUARY 12

FEBRUARY 13

*I*t was God...who made the
garden grow in your hearts.

1 Corinthians 3:6 TLB

$\mathcal{I}$ am yours, you are mine.
Of this we are certain.
You are lodged in my heart,
the small key is lost.
You must stay there forever.

FRAU AVA

FEBRUARY 14

February 15

At the end of your life you will never regret not having passed one more test, not winning one more verdict, or not closing one more deal. You will regret time not spent with a husband, a friend, a child, or a parent.

Barbara Bush

$\mathcal{B}$lessed are those who
can give without remembering,
and take without forgetting.

ELIZABETH BIBESCO

FEBRUARY 16

FEBRUARY 17

A family is a little world
created by love.

$\mathcal{I}$ believe in the sun even
when it is not shining. I believe in
love even when I do not feel it.
I believe in God even
when He is silent.

FEBRUARY 18

FEBRUARY 19

*Y*our heavenly Father
knows your needs. He will
always give you all you
need from day to day.

LUKE 12:30-31 TLB

S ometimes I must drive
her crazy. But she loves me anyway
and never lets on. She continues to
guard my heart and nurture my soul.
My sister is a true blessing in my life.

BETTY PEARL HOOPER

FEBRUARY 20

FEBRUARY 21

*T*hank you for believing in me
before I believed in myself.

$\mathcal{I}$ don't dream of wealth
and success for you. But instead,
a job you like, skills you can perfect,
enthusiasms to lighten your heart,
friends, and love in abundance.

PAM BROWN

FEBRUARY 22

FEBRUARY 23

Love loves to be told what
it knows already.... It wants to be
asked for what it longs to give.

P. T. FORSYTH

$\mathcal{D}$o not withhold good from
those who deserve it, when it is
in your power to act.

PROVERBS 3:27 NIV

FEBRUARY 24

FEBRUARY 25

*O*ther things may change us,
but we start and end with family.

ANTHONY BRANDT

$\mathcal{W}$hen you are truly
joined in spirit, another woman's
good is your good too.
Your work for the good
of each other.

RUTH SENTER

FEBRUARY 26

FEBRUARY 27

*God's fingers can touch
nothing but to mold it into loveliness.*

GEORGE MACDONALD

$\mathcal{C}$ontentment is not the
fulfillment of what you want,
but the realization of
how much you already have.

FEBRUARY 28

FEBRUARY 29

Whatever is true, whatever
is noble, whatever is right, whatever
is pure, whatever is lovely, whatever is
admirable—if anything is excellent or
praiseworthy—think about such things.

PHILIPPIANS 4:8 NIV

$\mathcal{M}$y sister is my heart.
She opens doors to rooms
I never knew were there,
Breaks through walls
I don't recall building.
She lights my darkest corners
With the sparkle in her eyes.

LISA LORDEN

MARCH 1

MARCH 2

Your greatest pleasure
is that which rebounds from
hearts that you have made glad.

HENRY WARD BEECHER

*W*hen you look at your life,
the greatest happinesses are
family happinesses.

JOYCE BROTHERS

MARCH 3

MARCH 4

*G*od loves each one
of us as if there
were only one of us.

AUGUSTINE

$\mathcal{T}$his is the day
the Lord has made.
We will rejoice and
be glad in it.

PSALM 118:24 TLB

MARCH 5

MARCH 6

$\mathcal{I}$ live for those who love me,
Whose hearts are kind and true,
For the human ties that bind me,
For the task by God assigned me,
For the bright hopes left behind me,
And the good that I can do.

GEORGE L. BANKS

$\mathcal{G}$o to the effort. Invest the
time. Write the letter.
Make the apology. Take the trip.
Purchase the gift. Do it. The
seized opportunity renders joy.

MAX LUCADO

MARCH 7

MARCH 8

*M*ay the warming love
of friends surround you as you go,
Down the path of light and laughter
where the happy memories grow.

HELEN LOWRIE MARSHALL

$\mathcal{T}$o know someone here
or there with whom you feel there
is an understanding in spite of distances
or thoughts unexpressed—that can
make of this earth a garden.

GOETHE

MARCH 9

MARCH 10

*B*ecause the Lord is
my Shepherd, I have everything
I need! He lets me rest in the meadow
grass and leads me beside
the quiet streams.
He gives me new strength.

PSALM 23:1-3 TLB

$\mathcal{H}$aving a sister is
like having a best friend you
can't get rid of. You know
whatever you do, they'll
still be there.

AMY LI

MARCH 11

MARCH 12

*T*he real joy of life is in its play.
Play is anything we do for the joy
and love of doing it.

WALTER RAUSCHENBUSCH

$\mathcal{I}$t is the family that gives us a
deep private sense of belonging.
Here we first begin to have
our self defined for us.

HOWARD THURMAN

MARCH 13

MARCH 14

$\mathcal{G}$od has made His children
by adoption nearer to Himself
than the angels.

THOMAS WATSON

$\mathcal{W}$herever your treasure
is, there your heart and
thoughts will be also.

LUKE 12:34 TLB

MARCH 15

MARCH 16

$\mathscr{C}$hance made us sisters,
Hearts made us friends.

$\mathcal{H}$appy is the person
who knows what to remember
of the past, what to enjoy
in the present, and what to
plan for the future.

A. GLASON

MARCH 17

MARCH 18

*O*h, the comfort—the inexpressible
comfort of feeling safe with a person—
having neither to weigh thoughts nor
measure words, but pouring them all right
out, just as they are, chaff and grain
together; certain that a faithful hand will
take and sift them, keep what is worth
keeping, and then with the breath of
kindness blow the rest away.

DINAH MARIA MULOCK CRAIK

$\mathcal{W}$e do not understand
the intricate pattern of the stars
in their courses, but we know that
He who created them does, and
that just as surely as He guides them,
He is charting a safe course for us.

BILLY GRAHAM

MARCH 19

MARCH 20

*H*e surrounds me with
loving-kindness and tender mercies.
He fills my life with good things!

PSALM 103:4-5 TLB

$\mathcal{A}$ sister is dear to you
always, for she is someone who
is always a part of all the favorite
memories that you keep very
close to your heart.

MARCH 21

MARCH 22

Among God's best gifts to us
are the people who love us.

*Z*ife is short and we never
have enough time for gladdening
the hearts of those who travel
the way with us. O, be swift to love!
Make haste to be kind.

HENRI FRÉDÉRIC AMIEL

MARCH 23

MARCH 24

*K*ind words are jewels
that live in the heart and soul
and remain as blessed memories
years after they have
been spoken.

MARVEA JOHNSON

$\mathcal{B}$e full of sympathy toward
each other, loving one another
with tender hearts and
humble minds.

1 Peter 3:8 tlb

MARCH 25

MARCH 26

*T*hank you, Father, for the beautiful
surprises you are planning for me today.
So often in my life...an unexpected burst
of golden sunshine has exploded through
a black cloud, sending inspiring shafts of
warm, beautiful sunshine into my life.

ROBERT SCHULLER

$\mathcal{T}$he great acts of love
are done by those who are
habitually performing small
acts of kindness.

MARCH 27

MARCH 28

*R*each out and care for
someone who needs the touch of
hospitality. The time you spend
caring today will be a love gift
that will blossom into the fresh
joy of God's Spirit in the future.

EMILIE BARNES

$\mathcal{M}$y sister is my past.
She writes my history
In her eyes I recognize myself,
Memories only we can share.
She remembers, she forgives
She accepts me as I am
With tender understanding.

LISA LORDEN

MARCH 29

MARCH 30

I know what it is to be in
need, and I know what it is
to have plenty. I have learned
the secret of being content in
any and every situation.

PHILIPPIANS 4:12 NIV

Some people make the
world special just by being in it.

MARCH 31

APRIL 1

$\mathcal{S}$ometimes our light goes
out but is blown into flame by
another human being. Each of us
owes deepest thanks to those
who have rekindled this light.

ALBERT SCHWEITZER

$\mathcal{I}$f instead of a gem, or
even a flower, we should cast
the gift of a loving thought into the
heart of a friend, that would be
giving as the angels give.

GEORGE MACDONALD

APRIL 2

APRIL 3

$\mathcal{A}$ sister is both your
mirror—and your opposite.

ELIZABETH FISHEL

$\mathcal{B}$e beautiful inside,
in your hearts, with the lasting
charm of a gentle and quiet spirit
which is so precious to God.

1 Peter 3:4 TLB

April 4

APRIL 5

*E*very time we encourage
someone, we give them a
transfusion of courage.

CHARLES SWINDOLL

*B*lue skies with white clouds
on summer days. A myriad of stars
on clear moonlit nights.... Bluebirds and
laughter and sunshine and Easter.
See how He loves us!

ALICE CHAPIN

APRIL 6

APRIL 7

*T*he best things are nearest:
breath in your nostrils, light in your
eyes, flowers at your feet, duties
at your hand, the path of God
just before you.

ROBERT LOUIS STEVENSON

$\mathcal{T}$ake a moment to recall
a time when you really felt loved.
When there was no question in
your mind about being loved for
just who you are. That is how
God loves you every single day.

APRIL 8

APRIL 9

$\mathcal{I}$ will not forget you.
See, I have inscribed you on
the palms of my hands.

Isaiah 49:15-16 NRSV

My sister's hands are fair and white;
my sister's hands are dark
My sister's hands are touched with age,
or by the years unmarked
And often when I pray for strength
to live as He commands
The Father sends me sustenance
in my sister's hands.

APRIL 10

APRIL 11

*T*he human heart,
at whatever age,
opens only to the heart
that opens in return.

Maria Edgeworth

$\mathcal{W}$ho we are is connected
to those we love and to
those who have influenced
us toward goodness.

CHRISTOPHER DE VINCK

APRIL 12

APRIL 13

*L*aughing at ourselves as
well as with each other gives a
surprising sense of togetherness.

HAZEL C. LEE

$\mathcal{I}$ will send down showers
in season; there will be
showers of blessing.

EZEKIEL 34:26 NIV

APRIL 14

APRIL 15

$\mathcal{T}$he wonder of living is held
within the beauty of silence, the glory
of sunlight...the sweetness of fresh
spring air, the quiet strength of earth,
and the love that lies at the
very root of all things.

$\mathcal{W}$e are not called
by God to do extraordinary
things, but to do ordinary things
with extraordinary love.

JEAN VANIER

APRIL 16

APRIL 17

*T*he supreme happiness
of life is the conviction
that we are loved.

VICTOR HUGO

The best friendships have weathered misunderstandings and trying times. One of the secrets of a good relationship is the ability to accept the storms.

ALAN LOY MCGINNIS

APRIL 18

APRIL 19

*D*on't be weary in prayer;
keep at it; watch for God's answers,
and remember to be thankful
when they come.

COLOSSIANS 4:2 TLB

My sisters have taught
me how to live.

GEORGE WASSERSTEIN

APRIL 20

APRIL 21

*T*he really great person
is the one who makes
everyone feel great.

G. K. CHESTERTON

$\mathcal{T}$o feel love gives pleasure
to one; to express it gives
pleasure to two.

JANETTE OKE

APRIL 22

APRIL 23

Wholehearted, ready laughter heals, encourages, relaxes anyone within hearing distance. The laughter that springs from love makes wide the space around it—gives room for the loved one to enter in.

EUGENIA PRICE

So don't be anxious
for tomorrow. God will take
care of your tomorrow too.
Live one day at a time.

MATTHEW 6:34 TLB

APRIL 24

APRIL 25

A sister is one of the nicest things that can happen to anyone. She is someone to laugh with and share with, to work with and join in the fun. She is someone who helps in the rough times and knows when you need a warm smile. She is someone who will quietly listen when you just want to talk for awhile.

$\mathcal{T}$uck [this] thought into
your heart today. Treasure it.
Your Father God cares about your
daily everythings that concern you.

Kay Arthur

April 26

APRIL 27

$\mathcal{A}$ family is a group of individuals
who are related to one another by
marriage, birth, or adoption—nothing more,
nothing else. This is not merely human
in origin. It is God's marvelous creation.

JAMES DOBSON

$\mathcal{W}$hen seeds of kindness
are sown prayerfully in the garden
plot of our lives, we may be sure
that there will be a bountiful harvest
of blessings for both us and others.

W. PHILLIP KELLER

APRIL 28

APRIL 29

*T*he winter is past;
the rains are over and gone.
Flowers appear on the earth;
the season of singing has come.

SONG OF SONGS 2:11-12 NIV

$\mathcal{H}$ow do people make
it through life without a sister?

SARA CORPENING

APRIL 30

MAY 1

*T*oday well lived makes
every yesterday a dream
of happiness and every
tomorrow a vision of hope.

$\mathcal{I}$ am glad that in the
springtime of life there were
those who planted flowers
of love in my heart.

ROBERT LOUIS STEVENSON

MAY 2

MAY 3

*S*ilences make the real
conversations between friends.
Not the saying, but the never
needing to say is what counts.

MARGARET LEE RUNBECK

$\mathcal{T}$he Lord will guide you always;
he will satisfy your needs.... You will be
like a well-watered garden, like a
spring whose waters never fail.

ISAIAH 58:11 NIV

MAY 4

MAY 5

Live your life while
you have it. Life is a splendid
gift—there is nothing
small about it.

FLORENCE NIGHTINGALE

$\mathcal{I}$f your sister is in a
tearing hurry to go out and
cannot catch your eye,
she's wearing your best sweater.

PAM BROWN

MAY 6

MAY 7

_M_ay God give you
eyes to see beauty only
the heart can understand.

*T*he blossom cannot tell
what becomes of its fragrance
as it drifts away, just as no person
can tell what becomes of their
influence as they continue through life.

MAY 8

MAY 9

In quietness and trust
shall be your strength.

Isaiah 30:15 NIV

$\mathscr{C}$ease to inquire whatever
the future has in store, and take
as a gift whatever the
day brings forth.

HORACE

MAY 10

MAY 11

*S*isters touch your
heart in ways no other could.
Sisters share...their hopes, their fears,
their love, everything they have.
Real friendship springs from
their special bonds.

$\mathcal{Y}$ou are...infinitely dear
to the Father, unspeakably
precious to Him. You are never,
not for one second, alone.

NORMAN DOWTY

MAY 12

MAY 13

*G*od loves and cares for us,
even to the least event and
smallest need of life.

HENRY MANNING

$\mathcal{I}$ do not cease to give
thanks for you as I remember
you in my prayers.

EPHESIANS 1:16 NRSV

MAY 14

MAY 15

$\mathcal{L}$ove is pressing around us
on all sides like air. Cease to
resist it and instantly love
takes possession.

AMY CARMICHAEL

There's a special kind
of freedom sisters enjoy.
Freedom to share innermost
thoughts, to ask a favor, to show
their true feelings. The freedom
to simply be themselves.

MAY 16

MAY 17

*I*f I knew you and you knew me,
If both of us could clearly see,
And with an inner sight divine
The meaning of your heart and mine,
I'm sure that we would differ less,
And clasp our hands in friendliness;
Our thoughts would pleasantly agree
If I knew you and you knew me.

NIXON WATERMAN

$\mathcal{T}$he splendor of the
rose and the whiteness of the
lily do not rob the little violet of
its scent nor the daisy of its simple
charm. If every tiny flower wanted to
be a rose, spring would
lose its loveliness.

THÉRÈSE OF LISIEUX

MAY 18

MAY 19

*E*ncourage each other
to build each other up, just
as you are already doing.

1 Thessalonians 5:11 tlb

$\mathcal{L}$ove is reaching, touching and caring, sharing sunshine and flowers, so many happy hours together.

MAY 20

MAY 21

$\mathcal{I}$f I had a single flower
for every time I think of you,
I could walk forever in my garden.

CLAUDIA A. GRANDI

My sister is like no one else
She's my most treasured friend
Filling up the empty spaces
Healing broken places
She is my rock, my inspiration.
Though impossible to define,
In a word, she is...my sister.

LISA LORDEN

MAY 22

MAY 23

When we allow God the privilege of shaping our lives, we discover new depths of purpose and meaning.

JONI EARECKSON TADA

$\mathcal{Y}$ou created my inmost being;
you knit me together in my
mother's womb. I praise you because
I am fearfully and wonderfully made;
your works are wonderful,
I know that full well.

Psalm 139:13-14 NIV

MAY 24

MAY 25

*U*se what talents you
possess: the woods would be
very silent if no birds sang there
except those that sang best.

HENRY VAN DYKE

$\mathcal{H}$old fast your dreams!
Within your heart
Keep one still, secret spot
Where dreams may go
And sheltered so,
May thrive and grow....
O keep a place apart,
Within your heart,
For little dreams to go!

Louise Driscoll

May 26

MAY 27

Within each of us, just
waiting to blossom, is the wonderful
promise of all we can be.

One ought, every day
at least, to hear a little song,
read a good poem, see a fine picture,
and, if it were possible, to speak
a few reasonable words.

GOETHE

MAY 28

MAY 29

$\mathcal{I}$t takes wisdom to have
a good family, and it takes
understanding to make it strong.

PROVERBS 24:3 NCV

$\mathcal{S}$omeone to talk to, to laugh with, to tell secrets to... I'm just so thankful for the friend I've found in you.

MAY 30

MAY 31

*T*o be grateful is to recognize
the love of God in everything
He has given us—and He has given
us everything. Every breath we
draw is a gift of His love, every
moment of existence a gift of grace.

THOMAS MERTON

$\mathcal{I}$n a world where it is necessary
to succeed, perhaps...we women
know more deeply that success
can be a quiet and hidden thing.

PAM BROWN

JUNE 1

JUNE 2

*T*he important thing is this:
To be ready at any moment
to sacrifice what we are for
what we could become.

Charles DuBois

$\mathcal{F}$or he will command his
angels concerning you to
guard you in all your ways.

PSALM 91:11 NIV

JUNE 3

JUNE 4

A gentle word, like summer rain,
May soothe some heart and banish pain.
What joy or sadness often springs
From just the simple little things!

WILLA HOEY

$\mathcal{T}$he gift of friendship—both
given and received—is joy, love and
nurturing for the heart. The realization
that you have met a soul mate...a kindred
spirit...a sister...a true friend...is one
of life's sweetest gifts!

JUNE 5

JUNE 6

$\mathcal{A}$ kind heart is a fountain
of gladness, making everything in
its vicinity freshen into smiles.

WASHINGTON IRVING

$\mathcal{G}$od's peace is joy resting.
His joy is peace dancing.

F. F. BRUCE

JUNE 7

JUNE 8

$\mathcal{I}$f you love someone, you will
be loyal to them no matter
what the cost.

1 CORINTHIANS 13:7 TLB

$\mathcal{M}$ay you wake each day
with His blessings and sleep each
night in His keeping, and may you
always walk in His tender care.

JUNE 9

JUNE 10

*L*ike branches on a tree
we grow in different directions
yet our roots remain as one. Each of
our lives will always be a special
part of the other.

*P*ut your feet up.
Read the paper. Order dinner out.
Escape the ordinary for one day.
You've worked hard. You've taken
care of others all week.
Now take care of yourself.

JUNE 11

JUNE 12

$\mathcal{W}$ith kindness, the difficult
becomes easy...life assumes a charm
and its miseries are softened.

CHARLES WAGNER

$\mathscr{M}$ay the Lord keep watch
between you and me when we
are away from each other.

GENESIS 31:49 NIV

JUNE 13

JUNE 14

*W*hat you do when you
don't have to determines what
you will be when you can
no longer help it.

RUDYARD KIPLING

$\mathcal{M}$y sister is my strength
She hears the whispered prayers
That I cannot speak
She helps me find my smile,
Freely giving hers away
She catches my tears
In her gentle hands.

LISA LORDEN

JUNE 15

JUNE 16

*T*here is nothing more
magnetic or attractive
than your smile.

CHARLES SWINDOLL

$\mathcal{T}$ have held many things
in my hands, and I have lost them all;
but whatever I have placed in God's
hands, that I still possess.

MARTIN LUTHER

JUNE 17

JUNE 18

I pray that you may enjoy good health and that all may go well with you, even as your soul is getting along well.

3 JOHN 1:2 NIV

$\mathcal{I}$t isn't great big pleasures
that count the most; it's making
a great deal out of the little ones.

JEAN WEBSTER

JUNE 19

JUNE 20

It's as if we are cut from the same fabric. Even though we appear to be sewn in a different pattern, we have a common thread that won't be broken—by people or years or distance.

$\mathcal{W}$e all mold one
another's dreams.
We all hold each other's
fragile hopes in our hands.
We all touch others' hearts.

JUNE 21

JUNE 22

$\mathcal{I}$ asked God for all things
that I might enjoy life. He gave
me life that I might enjoy all things.

$\mathcal{L}$ive out your God-created
identity. Live generously and
graciously toward others, the way
God lives toward you.

MATTHEW 5:48 THE MESSAGE

JUNE 23

JUNE 24

*G*ive what you have.
To someone it may be better
than you dare to think.

LONGFELLOW

$\mathcal{M}$ore and more I realize
that everybody, regardless of age,
needs to be hugged and comforted
in a brotherly or sisterly way now
and then. Preferably now.

JANE HOWARD

JUNE 25

JUNE 26

*T*he beauty of a woman is
not in the clothes she wears,
The figure that she carries, or the
way she combs her hair.
The beauty of a woman must be
seen from in her eyes,
Because that is the doorway to her heart,
the place where love resides.

AUDREY HEPBURN

$\mathcal{T}$he greatest gift we
can give one another
is rapt attention to one
another's existence.

SUE ATCHLEY EBAUGH

JUNE 27

JUNE 28

*E*mbrace this God-life.
Really embrace it, and nothing will
be too much for you.... That's why I
urge you to pray for absolutely
everything, ranging from small to large.
Include everything as you embrace
this God-life, and you'll get
God's everything.

MARK 11:22-24 THE MESSAGE

$\mathcal{I}$n all ranks of life the
human heart yearns for the
beautiful; and the beautiful things
that God makes are
His gift to all alike.

HARRIET BEECHER STOWE

JUNE 29

JUNE 30

What surprised me was
that within a family, the voices of
sisters as they're talking are
virtually always the same.

ELIZABETH FISHEL

$\mathcal{I}$t's nice to know there is someone you can tell everything to, and they'll still like you when you're done.

JULY 1

JULY 2

Sometimes it is a slender thread,
Sometimes a strong, stout rope;
She clings to one end,
I the other;
She calls it friendship;
I call it hope.

LOIS WYSE

$\mathcal{T}$he Lord longs to
be gracious to you; he rises
to show you compassion.

ISAIAH 30:18 NIV

JULY 3

JULY 4

*Y*ou are valuable just
because you exist. Not because
of what you do or what you have
done, but simply because you are.

MAX LUCADO

$\mathcal{K}$indness opens in
each heart a little heaven.

JULY 5

JULY 6

We have something precious.
I am reminded of that whenever
I am away from you, busy doing
something, and you drift into my
mind, making me smile inside.

GARRY LAFOLLETTE

$\mathcal{B}$e patient with
yourself and others.
Growing fruit takes time.

JULY 7

JULY 8

*T*here is far more to your
inner life than the food you put in
your stomach, more to your outer
appearance than the clothes you hang
on your body. Look at the ravens, free
and unfettered, not tied down to a
job description, carefree in the care
of God. And you count far more.

LUKE 12:22-23 THE MESSAGE

*G*od will never let you
be shaken or moved from your
place near His heart.

JULY 9

JULY 10

$\mathcal{K}$indness is given so softly, so gently,
Falling like tiny seeds along our paths—and
brightening them with flowers.

PAM BROWN

$\mathcal{L}$ove feels no burden,
thinks nothing of trouble,
attempts what is above its
strength, pleads no excuse
of impossibility.

THOMAS À KEMPIS

JULY 11

JULY 12

*G*ood company on a
journey makes the way to
seem all the shorter.

IZAAK WALTON

$\mathcal{I}$f you give, you will get!
Your gift will return to you in full
and overflowing measure, pressed
down, shaken together to make
room for more, and running over.

LUKE 6:38 TLB

JULY 13

JULY 14

*L*ove has been called
the most effective motivational
force in all the world. When love
is at work in us, it is remarkable
how giving and forgiving, understanding
and tolerant we can be.

CHARLES SWINDOLL

$\mathscr{T}$he desire to be and have a sister is a primitive and profound one that may have everything or nothing to do with the family a woman is born to. It is a desire to know and be known by someone who shares blood and body, history and dreams, common ground and the unknown adventures of the future, darkest secrets and the glassiest beads of truth.

ELIZABETH FISHEL

JULY 15

JULY 16

Z ife is God's gift to you.
The way you live your life
is your gift to God.
Make it a fantastic one.

LEO BUSCAGLIA

$\mathcal{A}$ smile costs nothing
but gives much. It takes but a
moment, but the memory of it
sometimes lasts forever.

JULY 17

JULY 18

$\mathcal{L}$ove one another the way
I loved you. This is the very best
way to love. Put your life on
the line for your friends.

JOHN 15:12-13 THE MESSAGE

$\mathcal{I}$ still find each day too short
for all the thoughts I want to think,
all the walks I want to take, all the books
I want to read, and all the friends I
want to see. The longer I live,
the more my mind dwells upon
the beauty and the wonder
of the world.

JOHN BURROUGHS

JULY 19

JULY 20

*M*y sister taught me
everything I really need to know,
and she was only in sixth
grade at the time.

*E*very day in a life fills
the whole life with expectation
and memory.

C. S. Lewis

July 21

JULY 22

*I*t is the simple things of
life that make living worthwhile,
the sweet fundamental things such
as love and duty, work and rest,
and living close to nature.

LAURA INGALLS WILDER

$\mathcal{W}$ithout God, it is
utterly impossible. But with
God everything is possible.

MARK 10:27 TLB

JULY 23

JULY 24

*G*od's gifts put man's
best dreams to shame.

ELIZABETH BARRETT BROWNING

$\mathcal{A}$ sister is one who knows
you as you really are, understands
where you've been, accepts
who you've become, and still
gently invites you to grow.

JULY 25

JULY 26

*T*oday, see if you can stretch
your heart and expand your love
so that it touches not only those
to whom you can give it easily, but
also those who need it so much.

DAPHNE ROSE KINGMA

$\mathcal{A}$ great woman is she
who has not lost the
heart of a child.

JULY 27

JULY 28

*T*his is my prayer: that your love will flourish and that you will not only love much but well. Learn to love appropriately. You need to use your head and test your feelings so that your love is sincere and intelligent.

PHILIPPIANS 1:9 10 THE MESSAGE

$\mathcal{P}$utting an emotion into
words gives it a life and a
reality that otherwise it doesn't have....
Similarly, expressing confidence
in a person's ability to accomplish
something actually strengthens
that ability.

ARTHUR GORDON

JULY 29

JULY 30

If I could reach up and
hold a star for every time you've
made me smile, the entire
evening sky would be in
the palm of my hand.

$\mathcal{I}$ wished I had a box,
the biggest I could find,
I'd fill it right up to the brim with
everything that's kind.
A box without a lock, of course,
and never any key;
for everything inside that box
would then be offered free.
Grateful words for joys received
I'd freely give away.
Oh, let us open wide a box
of praise for every day.

JULY 31

AUGUST 1

$\mathcal{A}$ friend is someone who understands your past, believes in your future, and accepts you today just the way you are.

BEVERLY LAHAYE

$\mathcal{I}$ will lie down and sleep
in peace, for you alone, O Lord,
make me dwell in safety.

PSALM 4:8 NIV

AUGUST 2

AUGUST 3

God is so big He can cover
the whole world with His love,
and so small He can curl up
inside your heart.

JUNE MASTERS BACHER

$\mathcal{L}$oving relationships are
a family's best protection against
the challenges of the world.

B. WIEBE

AUGUST 4

AUGUST 5

If you treat an individual
as if she were what she ought
to be and could be, she will
become what she ought to
be and could be.

$\mathcal{I}$ find that as I grow older,
I love those most whom I loved first.

THOMAS JEFFERSON

AUGUST 6

August 7

May the Lord bless and protect you; may the Lord's face radiate with joy because of you; may he be gracious to you, show you his favor, and give you his peace.

NUMBERS 6:24-26 TLB

$\mathcal{W}$e are each other's
reference point at
our turning points.

ELIZABETH FISHEL

AUGUST 8

AUGUST 9

*B*eing sisters is probably
the most competitive relationship
within the family, but once the
sisters are grown, it becomes the
strongest relationship.

MARGARET MEAD

$\mathcal{T}$he secret of life is that
all that we have and are is a
gift of grace to be shared.

LLOYD JOHN OGILVIE

AUGUST 10

AUGUST 11

Love puts the fun in together...
the sad in apart...
the hope in tomorrow...
the joy in a heart.

$\mathcal{E}$very path he guides us
on is fragrant with his loving-kindness
and his truth.

PSALM 25:10 TLB

AUGUST 12

AUGUST 13

*E*very house where
love abides and friendship is
a guest is surely home, and home
sweet home; for there
the heart can rest.

HENRY VAN DYKE

$\mathcal{M}$y sister hears the song
in my heart and sings it to me
when my memory fails.

AUGUST 14

AUGUST 15

*H*ow beautiful a day can be
when kindness touches it.

GEORGE ELLISTON

Originality is not doing something no one else has ever done, but doing what has been done countless times with new life, new breath.

MARIE CHAPIAN

AUGUST 16

August 17

*T*hose who hope in the
Lord will renew their strength.
They will soar on wings like eagles;
they will run and not grow weary,
they will walk and not be faint.

ISAIAH 40:31 NIV

$\mathscr{G}$od is not too great to
be concerned about
our smallest wishes.

BASILEA SCHLINK

AUGUST 18

AUGUST 19

$\mathcal{Y}$ou don't choose your family.
They are God's gift to you,
as you are to them.

DESMOND M. TUTU

Some days, it is enough encouragement just to watch the clouds break up and disappear, leaving behind a blue patch of sky and bright sunshine that is so warm upon my face. It's a glimpse of divinity; a kiss from heaven.

AUGUST 20

AUGUST 21

We are so very rich
if we know just a few people
in a way in which we
know no others.

CATHERINE BRAMWELL-BOOTH

I thank my God every time
I remember you. In all my prayers
for all of you, I always pray with joy.

Philippians 1:3-4 niv

August 22

AUGUST 23

*T*he next best thing
to being wise oneself is to live
in a circle of those who are.

C. S. LEWIS

$\mathcal{M}$ay God's love guide you
through the special plans
He has for your life.

AUGUST 24

AUGUST 25

As summer brings the happy times
The autumn winds will whisper
A closer friend I'd never find
Than the one I call my Sister.

VERNON

$\mathcal{I}$ know of no realm of life
that can provide more companionship
in a lonely world or greater feelings
of security and purpose in chaotic
times than the close ties of a family.

CHARLES SWINDOLL

AUGUST 26

AUGUST 27

*P*erfume and incense
bring joy to the heart,
and the pleasantness
of one's friend springs
from his earnest counsel.

PROVERBS 27:9 NIV

*O*ver all the mountaintops
is peace. In all treetops
you perceive scarcely a
breath. The little birds
in the forest are silent.
Wait then, soon you, too,
will have peace.

GOETHE

AUGUST 28

AUGUST 29

True friendships are lasting
because true love is eternal.
A friendship in which heart speaks
to heart is a gift from God, and no
gift that comes from God is
temporary or occasional.

HENRI J. M. NOUWEN

*G*ood communication is
as stimulating as black coffee,
and just as hard to sleep after.

ANNE MORROW LINDBERGH

AUGUST 30

AUGUST 31

*O*pen your hearts to the
love God instills.... God loves
you tenderly. What He gives you
is not to be kept under lock and key,
but to be shared.

MOTHER TERESA

$\mathscr{A}$ cheerful heart
is good medicine.

PROVERBS 17:22 NIV

SEPTEMBER 1

SEPTEMBER 2

*S*ince you are like no other
being ever created since the
beginning of time,
you are incomparable.

BRENDA UELAND

$\mathcal{T}$ake time to laugh,
it is the music of the soul.

SEPTEMBER 3

September 4

Love makes burdens lighter,
because you divide them.
It makes joys more intense,
because you share them.
It makes you stronger,
so that you can reach out and
become involved with life
in ways you dared not risk alone.

$\mathcal{L}$ove has a short memory.
It needs continual reminders.

LARRY CHRISTENSON

SEPTEMBER 5

SEPTEMBER 6

What happens when we live God's way? He brings gifts into our lives, much the same way that fruit appears in an orchard—things like affection for others, exuberance about life, serenity.

GALATIANS 5:22-23 THE MESSAGE

$\mathcal{H}$appiness always looks
small while you hold it
in your hands, but let it go,
and you learn at once
how big and precious it is.

SEPTEMBER 7

SEPTEMBER 8

$\mathcal{A}$ wonderful sister,
a special friend, that's what
you've been to me...so much
a part of lovely times
I keep in memory.

$\mathcal{W}$e are shaped and
fashioned by what we love.

GOETHE

SEPTEMBER 9

SEPTEMBER 10

$\mathcal{G}$od knows the rhythm of my spirit
and knows my heart thoughts.
He is as close as breathing.

*T*ake your everyday, ordinary
life—your sleeping, eating, going-to-work,
and walking-around life—and place
it before God as an offering.
Embracing what God does for you
is the best thing you can do for him.

ROMANS 12:1 THE MESSAGE

SEPTEMBER 11

September 12

*H*appiness is being at peace; being with loved ones; being comfortable.... But most of all, it's having those loved ones.

JOHNNY CASH

$\mathcal{L}$ove...comes out of heaven,
unasked and unsought.

PEARL S. BUCK

SEPTEMBER 13

SEPTEMBER 14

$\mathcal{I}$ do not ask for any crown
But that which all may win;
Nor try to conquer any world
Except the one within.

$\mathcal{R}$ecall it as often as you wish,
a happy memory never wears out.

LIBBIE FUDIM

SEPTEMBER 15

September 16

*Y*ou're blessed when you care.
At the moment of being "care-full,"
you find yourselves cared for.
You're blessed when you get your
inside world—your mind and heart—
put right. Then you can see God
in the outside world.

MATTHEW 5:7-8 THE MESSAGE

*I*f we celebrate the years
behind us they become stepping
stones of strength and joy
for the years ahead.

SEPTEMBER 17

September 18

The moments I love best are
the times I spend with you.

*Y*ou know as well as I do
the value of sisters' affections
to each other; there is nothing
like it in this world.

SEPTEMBER 19

September 20

*O*ur family is a unit that is not
shared by everyone. It is ours
by design, by tradition, by growth.
We love and protect it in our
own special way.

Janette Oke

Our God gives you everything
you need, makes you everything
you're to be.

2 Thessalonians 1:2 the mess

September 21

September 22

A good friend is a connection
to life—a tie to the past, a road
to the future, the key to sanity
in a totally insane world.

LOIS WYSE

$\mathcal{L}$ove has its source in
God, for love is the very
essence of His being.

KAY ARTHUR

SEPTEMBER 23

September 24

*T*he beauty of a woman is not
in a facial mole,
But true beauty in a woman is
reflected in her soul.
It is the caring that she lovingly gives,
the passion that she shows,
And the beauty of a woman with
passing years—only grows!

AUDREY HEPBURN

$\mathcal{T}$here is no time
like the old time, when you
and I were young!

OLIVER WENDELL HOLMES

SEPTEMBER 25

SEPTEMBER 26

May the God of hope fill you
with all joy and peace as you trust in him,
so that you may overflow with hope.

ROMANS 15:13 NIV

Sisters have one soul
between them.

SEPTEMBER 27

September 28

How dear to the heart
are the scenes of my childhood,
when fond recollection presents
them to view.

Samuel Woodworth

$\mathcal{D}$on't ever forget
that I will always love you!

SEPTEMBER 29

SEPTEMBER 30

*U*nhappiness does
not necessarily come from not
having this or that. If we have
each other, we have everything.

MOTHER TERESA

$\mathcal{B}$e completely humble
and gentle; be patient, bearing
with one another in love.

EPHESIANS 4:2 NIV

OCTOBER 1

OCTOBER 2

*O*nly He who created the
wonders of the world entwines
hearts in an eternal way.

$\mathcal{I}$ thank God, my friend,
for the blessing you are...for the
joy of your laughter...the comfort
of your prayers...the warmth
of your smile.

OCTOBER 3

OCTOBER 4

*S*isters are our peers,
the voice of our times.

ELIZABETH FISHEL

*A*nything, everything,
little or big becomes an
adventure when the right
person shares it.

KATHLEEN NORRIS

OCTOBER 5

OCTOBER 6

*D*ear friends, let us
practice loving each other,
for love comes from God and those
who are loving and kind show
that they are the children of God.

1 JOHN 4:7 TLB

$\mathcal{G}$od has a purpose for
your life and no one else can
take your place.

OCTOBER 7

OCTOBER 8

*H*eaven comes down
to touch us when we find ourselves
safe in the heart of another.

$\mathcal{L}$oving and being loved
is the greatest of human joys,
the ultimate human experience.
We can exist without love; but we
are not living fully as human
beings without it.

Edward E. Ford

October 9

OCTOBER 10

*Love is the true means
by which the world is enjoyed:
our love to others, and others'
love to us.*

THOMAS TRAHERNE

$\mathcal{Y}$ou are joined together
with peace through the Spirit,
so make every effort to
continue together in this way.

EPHESIANS 4:3 NCV

OCTOBER 11

OCTOBER 12

My sister often knows
the worst about me, but she
always believes in the best!

There is beauty in the forest
When the trees are green and fair,
There is beauty in the meadow
When the wildflowers scent the air.
There is beauty in the sunlight
and the soft blue beams above.
Oh, the world is full of beauty
when the heart is full of love.

OCTOBER 13

OCTOBER 14

*Y*ou have a unique message
to deliver, a unique song to sing,
a unique act of love to bestow.
This message, this song, and this act
of love have been entrusted exclusively
to the one and only you.

JOHN POWELL

$\mathcal{M}$y lifetime listens to yours.

MURIEL RUCKEYSER

OCTOBER 15

OCTOBER 16

*L*ord, you have examined
my heart and know everything about me....
You both precede and follow me, and
place your hand of blessing on my head.

PSALM 139:1,5 TLB

*O*ur family is a blessing.
It means so many things.
Words could never really tell
the joy our family brings....
Our family is heartfelt pride,
the feeling deep and strong,
That makes us glad to take a part
and know that we belong.

MARGARET FISHBACK POWERS

OCTOBER 17

OCTOBER 18

A sister listens to
your deepest hurts and
feels they are hers too.

Though I have seen the oceans and mountains, though I have read great books and seen great works of art, though I have heard symphonies and tasted the best...foods, there is nothing greater or more beautiful than those people I love.

CHRISTOPHER DE VINCK

OCTOBER 19

OCTOBER 20

$\mathcal{J}$t is a gift of God to us
to be able to share our
love with others.

MOTHER TERESA

$\mathcal{S}$ee to it that you really
do love each other warmly,
with all your hearts.

1 PETER 1:22 TLB

OCTOBER 21

OCTOBER 22

*D*ear Lord, please help me
to remember to take the time to
bestow the kisses today that I want
loved ones to remember tomorrow.

JENNIFER THOMAS

$\mathcal{A}$ sister is someone
who knows all about you,
and still chooses
not to go away.

OCTOBER 23

OCTOBER 24

*H*e made you so
you could share in His
creation, could love and
laugh and know Him.

TED GRIFFEN

$\mathcal{T}$reat your friends
like family and your
family like friends.

OCTOBER 25

OCTOBER 26

*L*ord...you have made known
to me the path of life; you will fill
me with joy in your presence, with
eternal pleasures at your right hand.

PSALM 16:5,11 NIV

$\mathcal{T}$he treasure our heart
searches for is found in
the ocean of God's love.

JANET L. WEAVER SMITH

OCTOBER 27

OCTOBER 28

'Tis the human touch in this
world that counts,
The touch of your hand on mine....
For shelter is gone when the night is o'er,
And bread lasts only a day,
But the touch of the hand and
the sound of the voice
Sing on in the soul always.

SPENCER MICHAEL FREE

*E*xpressed affection is
the best of all methods to use
when you want to light a glow
in someone's heart and to
feel it in your own.

RUTH STAFFORD PEALE

OCTOBER 29

OCTOBER 30

$\mathcal{Y}$ou will find as you look
back upon your life that the moments
when you have really lived are
the moments when you have done
things in the spirit of love.

HENRY DRUMMOND

$\mathcal{T}$he only thing that
counts is faith expressing
itself through love.

GALATIANS 5:6 NIV

OCTOBER 31

November 1

For whatever life holds for you and your family in the coming days, weave the unfailing fabric of God's Word through your heart and mind. It will hold strong, even if the rest of life unravels.

GIGI GRAHAM TCHIVIDJIAN

$\mathcal{T}$he fountain of beauty is
the heart, and every generous
thought illustrates the walls
of your chamber.

FRANCIS QUARLES

NOVEMBER 2

NOVEMBER 3

*B*oth within the family
and without, our sisters hold up
our mirrors, our images of
who we are and of who
we can dare to become.

ELIZABETH FISHEL

$\mathcal{O}$ur Creator would never
have made such lovely days, and
have given us the deep hearts
to enjoy them, above and
beyond all thought, unless
we were meant to be immortal.

NATHANIEL HAWTHORNE

NOVEMBER 4

NOVEMBER 5

When others are happy,
be happy with them. If they
are sad, share their sorrow.

ROMANS 12:15 TLB

$\mathcal{T}$hank you for the treasure
of your friendship...for showing
me God's special heart of love.

NOVEMBER 6

NOVEMBER 7

*T*here is nothing quite so
deeply satisfying as the solidarity
of a family united across the generations
and miles by a common faith and history.

SARA WENGER SHENK

$\mathcal{P}$eace within makes
beauty without.

ENGLISH PROVERB

NOVEMBER 8

NOVEMBER 9

$\mathcal{A}$ smile is the lighting system of the face and the heating system of the heart.

BARBARA JOHNSON

$\mathcal{L}$et love be your greatest aim.

1 CORINTHIANS 14:1 TLB

NOVEMBER 10

November 11

Can you measure the worth of a sunbeam,
  The worth of a treasured smile,
  The value of love and of giving,
The things that make life worthwhile?

ANNA GARNETT SCHULTZ

There are many people
who come and go in our lives....
A few touch us in ways that
change us forever, making us
better from knowing them.

NOVEMBER 12

November 13

*T*he happiest moments of
my life have been the few which
I have passed at home in the
bosom of my family.

THOMAS JEFFERSON

$\mathcal{L}$ove brings a new richness to life,
a higher intensity, a deeper meaning.

NOVEMBER 14

November 15

*G*ive thanks to the Lord,
for he is good; his love and
his kindness go on forever.

1 Chronicles 16:34 tlb

$\mathcal{H}$ow sweet the sound
of family laughing together,
of sharing the joy of knowing
each other so well.

NOVEMBER 16

NOVEMBER 17

*N*o one knows better than
a sister how we grew up, and
who our friends, teachers, and
favorite toys were. No one
knows better than she.

DALE V. ATKINS

$\mathcal{S}$eeing our Father in everything
makes life one long thanksgiving and
gives a rest of heart.

HANNAH WHITALL SMITH

NOVEMBER 18

November 19

*T*ake time to notice all
the usually unnoticed, simple
things in life. Delight in the
never-ending hope that's
available every day!

*T*hank the Lord for his steadfast love,
for his wonderful works to humankind.
For he satisfies the thirsty, and the
hungry he fills with good things.

PSALM 107:8-9 NRSV

NOVEMBER 20

NOVEMBER 21

$\mathscr{T}$hanksgiving is a time of quiet reflection
upon the past and an annual reminder
that God has, again, been ever so faithful.
The solid and simple things of life
are brought into clear focus.

CHARLES SWINDOLL

$\mathscr{N}$o one can develop
freely in this world and find a
full life without feeling understood
by at least one person.

PAUL TOURNIER

NOVEMBER 22

November 23

Gratitude. More aware of
what you have than what you don't.
Recognizing the treasure in the
simple—a child's hug, fertile soil,
a golden sunset. Relishing in the
comfort of the common.

$\mathcal{C}$all it a clan, call it a network,
call it a tribe, call it a family.
Whatever you call it, whoever
you are, you need one.

JANE HOWARD

NOVEMBER 24

NOVEMBER 25

*T*hanks be to God for
his indescribable gift!

2 CORINTHIANS 9:15 NIV

$\mathcal{G}$ratitude is a twofold
love—love coming to visit us
and love running out to greet
a welcome guest.

HENRY VAN DYKE

NOVEMBER 26

NOVEMBER 27

*W*hat families have in
common the world around is that
they are the place where people
learn who they are and
how to be that way.

JEAN ILLSLEY CLARK

$\mathcal{T}$he human contribution
is the essential ingredient.
It is only in the giving of oneself
to others that we truly live.

Ethel Percy Andrus

November 28

November 29

*T*o be rooted is perhaps the
most important and least
recognized need of the human soul.

SIMONE WEIL

$\mathcal{E}$very good and perfect
gift is from above, coming down
from the Father of the heavenly lights,
who does not change like
shifting shadows.

NOVEMBER 30

DECEMBER 1

*O*nly the heart knows how
to find what is precious.

FYODOR DOSTOYEVSKY

Often, in old age, [sisters] become each other's chosen and most happy companions. In addition to their shared memories of childhood and of their relationship to each other's children, they share memories of the same home, the same homemaking style, and the same small prejudices about housekeeping that carry the echoes of their mother's voice.

MARGARET MEAD

DECEMBER 2

DECEMBER 3

*G*ood times with you are
the best times in life.

$\mathcal{W}$e are each a secret
to the other. To know one
another means to feel mutual
affection and confidence, and to
believe in one another.

ALBERT SCHWEITZER

DECEMBER 4

DECEMBER 5

Love...binds everything together in perfect harmony.

$\mathcal{O}$ur sweetest experiences
of affection are meant to point
us to that realm which is the real
and endless home of the heart.

HENRY WARD BEECHER

DECEMBER 6

DECEMBER 7

*T*he hearts that love will
Know never winter's frost and chill.
Summer's warmth is in them still.

Eben Eugene Rexford

$\mathcal{T}$he healthiest relationships
are those that "breathe"—that is,
they move out from one another
for a few days and then come back
together for a time of closeness.

JAMES DOBSON

DECEMBER 8

DECEMBER 9

*S*isters—they share the agony
and the exhilaration. As youngsters
they may share popsicles, chewing gum,
hair dryers, and bedrooms. When they
grow up, they share confidences,
careers, and children, and some even
chat for hours every day.

ROXANNE BROWN

$\mathcal{T}$he Lord has done great things
for us, and we are filled with joy.

PSALM 126:3 NIV

DECEMBER 10

DECEMBER 11

*Y*our only treasures are
those which you carry in your heart.

DEMOPHILUS

$\mathcal{T}$he best and most beautiful things
in the world cannot be seen or even
touched. They must be felt with the heart.

HELEN KELLER

DECEMBER 12

DECEMBER 13

God's hand is always there,
once you grasp it you'll never
want to let it go.

$\mathcal{D}$on't walk in front of me,
I may not follow. Don't walk behind
me, I may not lead. Walk beside me
and just be my friend.

Albert Camus

December 14

DECEMBER 15

*E*very morning tell him,
"Thank you for your kindness,"
and every evening rejoice in
all his faithfulness.

PSALM 92:2 TLB

$\mathcal{T}$he most precious things
of life are near at hand.

JOHN BURROUGHS

DECEMBER 16

DECEMBER 17

*F*or attractive lips,
Speak words of kindness.
For lovely eyes,
Seek out the good in people.
For a slim figure,
Share your food with the hungry.
For beautiful hair,
Let a child run his or her fingers
through it once a day.
For poise,
Walk with the knowledge
you'll never walk alone.

AUDREY HEPBURN

$\mathcal{P}$eace is not a season,
it is a way of life.

DECEMBER 18

DECEMBER 19

*I*t is the season to be
jolly because, more than at any
other time, we think of Jesus.
More than in any other season,
His name is on our lips.

MAX LUCADO

"*The* virgin will be with child
and will give birth to a son,
and they will call him Immanuel"—which
means, "God with us."

MATTHEW 1:23 NIV

DECEMBER 20

December 21

The best gifts are tied
with heartstrings.

$\mathscr{C}$hristmas, my child,
is love in action.... Every time
we love, every time we give,
it's Christmas.

DALE EVANS ROGERS

DECEMBER 22

DECEMBER 23

My sister's love is very special,
one I'll treasure through the years.
We've played and laughed together
and ofttimes shed many tears.
but through life's maze of problems,
God placed a bond of love within
To unite our hearts in wisdom
changing sisters into friends.

JUDY MEGGERS

$\mathcal{G}$od grant you the light
in Christmas, which is faith;
the warmth of Christmas,
which is love...the all of
Christmas, which is Christ.

WILDA ENGLISH

DECEMBER 24

DECEMBER 25

*F*or to us a child is born,
to us a son is given, and the
government will be on his shoulders.
And he will be called Wonderful
Counselor, Mighty God, Everlasting
Father, Prince of Peace.

ISAIAH 9:6 NIV

$\mathcal{I}$t is good to be children
sometimes, and never better
than at Christmas, when its mighty
Founder was a child Himself.

CHARLES DICKENS

DECEMBER 26

DECEMBER 27

*T*aking joy in life is a
woman's best cosmetic.

ROSALIND RUSSELL

*C*herish your human connections:
your relationships with
friends and family.

BARBARA BUSH

DECEMBER 28

DECEMBER 29

*E*veryone has a unique role
to fill in the world and is important
in some respect. Everyone, including
and perhaps especially you,
is indispensable.

NATHANIEL HAWTHORNE

$\mathcal{M}$ay the Lord continually
bless you with heaven's blessings
as well as with human joys.

PSALM 128:5 TLB

DECEMBER 30

DECEMBER 31

*T*his new day brings
Another year,
Renewing hope...
Dispelling care.
And may we find
Before the end,
A deep content...
Another friend.